*This book is dedicated to my wonderful family who
I will always protect and keep safe.*

*I also dedicate this book to the brave men and women of our
armed forces and our law enforcement community.
Thank you for sacrificing so much for others.*

D0067268

Table of Contents

HANDGUN
FUNDAMENTALS
for the New Shooter

TOMMY SAPP

Introduction

This book is essential for anyone who aspires to carry a handgun. This book provides you with information to improve your skills and abilities as a handgun operator on the range, as well as in a self-defense scenario. Whether you are a novice or an experienced shooter, my techniques are stair-stepped to create good habits and break bad habits. If you carry a handgun for self-defense or defense of your loved ones, this book gives you the tools you need to win a violent encounter.

Who are you fighting for? Don't you owe it to yourself or those people to equip yourself with the ability to protect them from evil? You will always revert back to your training. Too many people rely on luck when it comes to self-defense. Allow me to elaborate and walk you through a typical gun fight. My hope is that you will never find yourself in a situation where you are forced to use your gun in self-defense.

Here's some possible scenarios. You are in a shopping center with your family picking up some back to school items when someone comes in firing off rounds and killing as many people as they can. Maybe you are just in the convenience store paying for your gas and an armed perpetrator comes in wearing a mask. Perhaps you are just stopped at a red light and someone decides to carjack you. There are hundreds of possibilities. If it happens, it will happen at an unknown location. It will take place on an unknown date and time. I always say it will happen when you expect it the least and to those who least expect it. Ironically, the one place where you are not likely to have to protect yourself is the gun range, which is the only place where most people carry a gun.

Next, you will be using an unknown skill. I seriously doubt that when you are encountered with a deadly threat that it will be just like you practiced at the range. That nice stance, closing one eye, lining up your sights, breathing calmly, and pressing that trigger straight to the rear. From experience I can tell you that you will likely be doing something you've never trained for before. You may be running backwards shooting with one hand, "spraying and praying." Or laying on the ground, hiding behind a car, or perhaps even pushing towards the threat. We do not know exactly how we will respond under such a large amount of stress. If we practice the fundamentals continuously then we are more likely to come out on top. More on that later.

Third, you have to have a clear understanding of the laws that govern use of force. You have to be able to articulate why you just shot at someone. Are you going to go to prison? Are you going to be sued? These questions must be asked and you don't have time for an internal debate when your life is on the line. I recommend that everyone who is going to carry a gun should study and be up to date on the laws that govern the use of deadly force.

Finally, what is most problematic is when the sympathetic nervous system kicks in. I'm talking about the fight or flight response. This is the body's response to an emergency, i.e. a deadly threat. Adrenaline dumps into your blood stream. Your heart rate increases and your blood pressure sky rockets. Your hands shake. You have auditory exclusion. The first time I was involved in a gun fight my partner was shooting and it sounded like a soft clap coming out of the end of the barrel. You will have visual exclusion, also known as tunnel vision. You can only focus on what's right in front of you. Fine motor skills are reduced, such as taking the gun off of safety. To top it off, your thinking brain or cognitive brain is reduced and you rely on your subconscious, also known as muscle memory. So to be able to draw and shoot accurately under these conditions you must train. If you don't train, you are relying on luck. So who are you fighting for? Is luck good enough for them? TRAIN!

With all of that being said, come into this book with an open mind. Try these proven techniques for yourself. If you try them and they aren't for you or you would rather shoot the way you've always shot, then trash them. But if these techniques add at least one tool in your toolbox, then it will be well worth the time it took to read it. My hope is that something you learn here could save your life or someone else's life. This book is about you, not me. While writing this book I had you in mind and I truly hope that it adds value to your handgun shooting.

Don't take my word for it. I encourage you to test my techniques at the range and make sure that they work for you. Reading this book doesn't make you a good shooter, you have to put some rounds downrange. I want you to become familiar with who is teaching you.

About Me

There are lots of "firearms instructors" out there who are creating bad habits. I believe their intentions are good, but nonetheless, some of the techniques that are being taught are nonsense. My background is in law enforcement; but, prior to entering the Police force I grew up in the woods of Florida walking around with a gun in my hand. I loved to shoot and I was always naturally good at it. I have been a Deputy Sheriff since 2005. It wasn't until about 2007 that I really decided to take my shooting to the next level. I decided to not just shoot, but to become proficient in shooting. I joined the SWAT team and became part of the training unit at the Sheriff's Office I worked at. There was a period of time where I was going to the range almost every single day. I wanted to be the best. I could run and shoot, shoot upside down, shoot quickly and shoot accurately. Then something shifted in my career. I became the SWAT team Commander and my role shifted from Operator to Teacher and Leader. I needed to become a great instructor and focus my attention into the art of instructing. My new role was to help others become better with their shooting. I became a Firearms instructor at the Police academy and started up two separate businesses teaching others to shoot firearms proficiently. Not only do I enjoy teaching others to shoot firearms (especially new shooters), I have discovered that it is a passion of mine. So what is the point to all of this? Am I just "tooting my own horn?" Not at all, I want you to know that I am not the best shooter in the world, I am not even as good as I used to be. One negative thing about teaching all of the time is that you lose a lot of your skills because you rarely get to shoot. I'm o.k. with that. I don't have to be the best shooter, but I strive to be the best Instructor in the world. How do I do that? By focusing on you and your needs and making you better and safer, that is what this book is about.

I hope that you enjoy this book and that it sets you up for success with a handgun. I will tell you what my training mentor always told me, "Train hard, fight easy!"

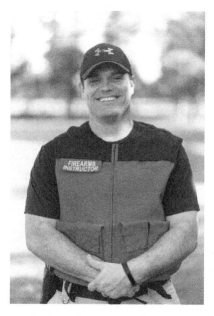

Tommy Sapp—Active Law Enforcement Officer,
Firearms Instructor, President of Focused Fire
Training LLC and Law Enforcement Advanced
Programs LLC (LEAP)

Chapter One
HANDGUN SAFETY

Entering into this handgun shooting venture, we have to discuss safety. Every time I start a training, whether it is with first time shooters or with seasoned SWAT personnel, I always do a safety briefing. If we are training all day and we leave for lunch, when we return to the range I do a second safety briefing. I do this so that these seven safety rules are fresh on the shooters mind as we begin to shoot. In my training career I have seen a handful of accidental discharges. I've even witnessed an accidental discharge during a SWAT standoff by a seasoned Sniper! It happens. If we will just follow these seven rules we can mitigate these occurrences and try to save a few lives.

RULE 1:
ALWAYS BE AWARE OF WHERE YOUR BARREL IS POINTING

Also known as having good "muzzle discipline", this rule has to be the most important rule of them all. When your weapon is out of the holster you have to be aware at all times of where that barrel is pointing. Here are a few examples of some of the incidents I have seen at the range.

I was teaching a basic handgun class to a group of new shooters. All of the students are in a line shooting downrange and we finish up a course of fire. I make sure everyone's safety is on and that their gun is holstered. Now it is break time. One of the students decides that he wants to show another student his gun during the break. As these two students are examining the gun and talking about it, I notice what is happening. The gun is pointed in the direction of the other students and myself. I immediately addressed this issue with the student and we did not have any further issues.

Another example that I have witnessed was during firearms training at a Police academy with cadets. One of the cadets had a weapons malfunction and instead of fixing the problem or raising her hand, she turned around with the gun and flagged every one of us behind her. She was not allowed to continue with the program.

Incidents like these happen all of the time! Some of them result in injury or death.

We ALWAYS have to be aware of where the barrel is pointing and it always has to be in a safe direction. Never point your weapon at anything that you are not willing to destroy.

RULE 2:
TRIGGER FINGER DISCIPLINE

Another important rule is to keep your finger off of the trigger until you're ready to fire. This means when you come out of the holster you have a straight finger, outside of the trigger guard. Your finger doesn't enter the trigger guard and onto the trigger until you are up on target. After discharging your rounds and before returning to the holster, your finger comes off of the trigger and back outside of the trigger guard.

Trigger Outside of the Trigger Guard

Straight Trigger Finger

Several years ago I was the SWAT Commander and I was in charge of a barricaded subject operation. The person had been held up inside of a home and we were in a standoff for nearly twelve hours. I had a Sniper placed in the rear of the residence in the wood line and he was providing intelligence and also providing cover. One of the team members was delivering waters to SWAT personnel who were holding the perimeter. He yelled out to the Sniper and threw him a bottle of water. The Sniper had his finger on the trigger as he reached up to catch the water. Have you ever heard of the sympathetic reflex? It basically means that whatever one hand does at one hundred percent, the other will do at fifty percent. Fifty percent on the trigger equaled boom! The high powered sniper rifle discharged five feet in front of where he was laying and all hell broke loose. Officers took cover and got on the radio yelling, "Shots fired, shots fired". You can imagine the embarrassment when the Sniper had to pipe up on the radio and say, "It was an accidental discharge". Luckily nobody was hurt in this case (except maybe the Sniper's pride). I've seen many accidental discharges occur because the operator had their finger on the trigger. So as the old saying goes, "keep your booger hook off of the bang stick" until you are ready to fire!

RULE 3:
TREAT ALL GUNS AS LOADED GUNS

This is a no brainer, yet we still see lots of accidental shootings happening all over the world. I recently watched a video where someone pointed what she thought was an unloaded gun at a friend and pulled the trigger. The weapon discharged and the friend took one round to the head. I can remember as a kid a friend of mine being killed by someone pointing an apparently "unloaded" gun at him and pulling the trigger. You absolutely have to treat every firearm as if it were loaded, even if you have safety checked it and know that it is empty.

RULE 4:
WEAR EYE AND EAR PROTECTION

You should at least be wearing sunglasses to the range, but I recommend shooting (safety) glasses. Hot brass can strike you in the eye. Fragmentation can strike you in the eye. Lots of bad things seem to happen when you don't follow the rules.

Hearing protection is a must! If you plan on spending any amount of time discharging firearms and you do not want to go deaf, make sure you wear your ear protection. For maximum protection wear soft ear plugs underneath electronic (amplified sound) ear muffs.

RULE 5:
ENSURE THAT YOU HAVE A SOLID BACKDROP

I like to ensure that I always have a solid backdrop when I am training. When I was growing up I would just fire rounds into the woods from my .30-30 rifle with no regard for anyone walking in the woods or how far that bullet may travel. I recommend a solid berm that will catch all of the projectiles that are fired.

You are responsible for every single round that comes out of that weapon. If you ever find yourself engaged in a deadly force situation where you have to fire your weapon at someone, please keep the backdrop principle in mind. If there is a group of people, a school, a grocery store, or anything that could be injured behind your target, you have to be considerate. You have to weigh the risks and decide if there are other options. If you absolutely must use your weapon, I hope that you have trained yourself to take that surgical shot under a large amount of stress.

RULE 6:
ENSURE THAT YOU HAVE PROPER TARGET IDENTIFICATION

When you are encountering a deadly threat in a real-life scenario, or even during training, I want you to visually process your target in the following progression. It always starts with the hands. Does he or she have a weapon? Then move to the waist band. Is there a weapon tucked away that I need to be aware of. Third, observe the subjects face and total demeanor. Is he or she aggressive? Does the subject look angry? Train yourself in every course of fire that you do to work through this visual progression so that in a real-life deadly force encounter it becomes second nature. The way you train is the way that you will perform.

RULE 7:
NO HORSEPLAY ON THE RANGE

I saved the best for last. No horseplay at the range. Period! Just because we are adults doesn't mean we will not play around. We get out to the range, we get comfortable, and sometimes we do things that are unsafe. It doesn't have to be horseplay. Sometimes a lack of focus after we get comfortable can cause us to have an accident.

I want to leave you with this final point on firearms safety. At the end of training is when you have to be completely focused. At the end of training we are tired, we are comfortable, and we are probably thinking about what we are going to be doing when we leave the range. This is where the accidents happen! This is where people are injured or killed because of a lack of focus. Train hard to the end, keep your focus, and everyone will leave the range with as many holes in their body as they came with.

RANGE SAFETY RULES

RULE 1
ALWAYS BE AWARE OF
WHERE YOUR BARREL IS POINTING

RULE 2
TRIGGER FINGER DISCIPLINE

RULE 3
TREAT ALL GUNS AS LOADED GUNS

RULE 4
WEAR EYE AND EAR PROTECTION

RULE 5
ENSURE THAT YOU
HAVE A SOLID BACKDROP

RULE 6
ENSURE THAT YOU HAVE
PROPER TARGET IDENTIFICATION

RULE 7
NO HORSEPLAY ON THE RANGE

Chapter 2
PROPER
FUNDAMENTALS

Train to Fight, Fight to Win!

In the training that I lead, even when that training is with advanced operators or military personnel, we always come back to the fundamentals. Sure it is more fun to have competitions, work on moving and shooting, and do the sexy stuff, but if you are not practicing the fundamentals then you are not training to win the fight. What you continuously do in training is what you will do in a fight. If you practice shooting with the incorrect fundamentals thousands of times, guess what? You will do it incorrectly when the sympathetic nervous system kicks in. So we need to train the proper fundamentals and we need to do it often.

As we dive into the fundamentals I have a small disclaimer. The fundamentals that I teach aren't for competition style shooting, although they will translate. These fundamentals are for the gun fight. These fundamentals are designed to give you the tactical advantage over your adversary and win the fight when your life is on the line. These are combat proven techniques!

I have provided photographs and drills to assist you with achieving mastery of these fundamentals. After mastering these techniques I encourage you to return to them in your training periodically to stay proficient. Lastly, if you try one of these techniques and you don't like it, scrap it. I don't claim to be the know-all when it comes to firearms training. I just want to share all of the knowledge that I have with you in hopes that you will have a few more tools for your toolbox.

Stance

This is the foundation of making accurate shots. To get into your stance you will be using gross motor skills, which as we have discussed may be all that you have available. The "old-school" weaver stance is out! The modified weaver stance is in only if you

Isosceles Stance – Top View

Isosceles Stance

have been doing it for so long that you won't feel comfortable changing it. I'm going to teach you the isosceles stance. To make this simple, when you are in the weaver stance one foot goes back and you are sideways, when you are in the isosceles stance you are squared off with your target.

When I am teaching firearms I always like to explain why we do what we do. With the weaver stance you lose some of your peripheral vision (15-30%) because you are turned sideways. You lose some of your recoil management ability because one arm is bent. Moving and shooting is more difficult because you have to walk sideways and cross your feet. In the weaver stance your natural point of aim is sideways instead of at the target. When your natural point of aim is one way, and the target is the other, you have to muscle your body towards your target. For law enforcement personnel, you want your body armor to be facing your target.

Let's get into the isosceles stance together: *Stand up, let's go!*

Start from the bottom always! Feet are shoulder width apart of slightly wider. Your weight is evenly distributed on the balls of your feet (you don't want to be flatfooted). Your knees are slightly bent. Press forward at the waist slightly (aggressive stance). Keep your head upright and your arms locked all the way out. When our arms are locked all the way out we are using joint support. When our arms are bent we are using muscle support. Joint support is much stronger and helps manage to the recoil of the gun.

A few pointers: We want a wide base so we are stable. We want knees bent and weight evenly distributed so that we can move if we need to. We want to slightly press forward to help manage recoil,

Modified Weaver Stance   *Weaver Stance*
                                    (Not Recommended)

but not too far. Bend forward at the waist until your nose is over your toes. Head upright. If you get into the stance and bring the gun up and have to kink your neck down to see the sights, you are putting unneeded pressure and strain on your body. Stay upright, stay comfortable, and bring the sights up to your eye level.

Grip
BASIC GRIP

I cannot stress enough the importance of maintaining a good grip. If you practice a good grip and it's built into your "muscle memory", then you will be a good shooter even if everything else is a little off. To start, grab the grip portion of your handgun with your dominant hand, also known as your "strong hand". Grab it like a baseball bat, wrapping your fingers all of the way around. Also make sure the web of your hand is as high as it will go. Next, wrap your non-dominant hand (also known as support hand) around the front of the dominant hand. Thumbs should run parallel along the slide facing the threat. Press out with your dominant hand and pull with your non-dominant hand. This creates enough tension so that when the weapon fires it should bring your sights back on targets. The tension helps you to manage the recoil and fire multiple rounds at a fast pace. Just to reiterate, your finger is off of the trigger until you are on target.

Basic Push/Pull Style Grip

TACTICAL GRIP

This grip is a little more advanced. I don't recommend this grip unless you are going to train regularly. You start this grip the same way with the dominant hand grabbing the pistol like a baseball bat. Drive the thumb of the support hand out and towards the target. Place as much of the support hand and thumb on the grip as possible. Instead of a push/pull tension, this grip allows you to sandwich the weapon in between your hands. The support hand thumb points at the target and can be used as a great point of reference for point shooting (more on this later) This grip also allows for you to maximize the amount of your hand that is on the weapon at all times which will assist with recoil management.

Support Hand Thumb Points at the Target. Below, tactical Pistol Grip

Head/Eye Position and Sight Alignment

One of the biggest issues with our stance is when we reach the top. Our tendency is to bring our heads down to the sights instead of bringing the gun up to our head. We put unnecessary tension on our neck which turns into more stress, more shakiness. We want to keep our head upright and relaxed and bring the sights of the gun up to our eye level as we have previously discussed.

Sight alignment is simple. Place the front sight in the middle of the two rear sights. You want the sights to be even or level across the top and have even spacing on the sides. You want to focus on your front sight. The rear sights should be slightly blurry and the target should be slightly blurry. The front sight should be crisp and clear. You can only truly focus on one thing at a time. Place the top of the sights wherever it is that you desire to impact and if all of the other mechanics are intact, then you should be accurate.

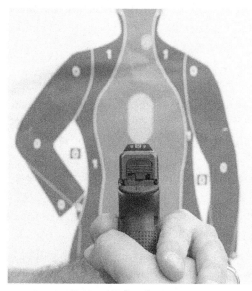

Proper Sight Alignment

23

Sights vs Point Shooting

Here's the truth. When your life is being threatened and your sympathetic nervous system kicks in a few things will happen. You will have an adrenaline dump, you will lose fine motor skills, and your heart rate will go through the roof! You revert to your caveman days and your cognitive thinking goes out the window (fight or flight response). You have auditory and visual exclusion (tunnel vision). With all of that going on is it likely that you will be lining up sights or just pointing and shooting? Obviously you will be point shooting. Are there surgical shots that need to be taken with proper sight alignment? Certainly. Is it nice to be able to hit the target with that nice four inch group at the range? Sure is. But in combat, you need to know how to point shoot properly. You need to know how to draw your gun without thinking, point it at the target without looking at the sights, and eliminate the threat. Also it is highly likely that you lose the ability to even close one eye and line up your sights because of the body's response to a threat. So here are my training recommendations for point shooting:

- Point shooting should take place at 7 yards and in.

- Point your straight trigger finger at the target, could you hit if a bullet came out of the end of your finger? It's that simple! You don't have to line your sights up to hit the target.

- Support hand thumb acts as a reference using the tactical pistol grip

- Look over the top of the gun to get a point of reference using your peripheral vision

- When you do your dry fire drills which will be covered in a later chapter, add at least ten dry fires of point shooting.

- Practice point shooting every time you go to the range. Keep both eyes open and do not use your sights. You can do this with a dry gun and a live gun.

Slack-Out Method over Trigger Reset

This is where it may get a little controversial. Most instructors teach you to use the trigger reset. So here is how that works. When you fire your first round, you keep the trigger depressed and slowly let it out until you hear and/or feel it click. When it clicks, the trigger is reset and it makes for a much shorter and much smoother trigger pull. This works great for target practice and marksmanship. This doesn't work so well for combat. Stress and the trigger reset function do not mix well.

With the slack out method, you let the slack back out of the trigger every time and take the full trigger pull. This technique only works well if you put at least a thousand rounds through your gun while practicing it. The trigger reset method is much easier to learn and to do correctly. It makes for smoother follow-up shots in a range setting, but not so much during a gun fight. The reason slack out works better is that finding that click by slowly easing the trigger out is a fine motor skill. Fine motor skills are out of the window when the fight or flight response kicks in. In a deadly force situation you don't have time to worry about finding that trigger reset. Additionally, the finger works faster pulling into you than it does extending out. So the slack out method is actually faster and more reliable if you practice!

Finger Placement/Trigger Pull

Proper trigger finger placement is essential to making accurate shots. You should place the trigger directly on the center of the pad of your index finger. If you put too much or too little finger on the trigger, it can change the trajectory of your rounds.

More importantly, you have to pull the trigger straight back to the rear of the gun. Most of the accuracy issues that I fix are when the shooter, especially the new shooter, "jerks" the trigger. The shooter knows that the gun is about to go off, and right before it does he or she anticipates the recoil and pushes the gun down. You have to pull that trigger straight back to the rear without anticipating the recoil of the gun using **steady and continuous pressure**. This comes with practice. The more you get comfortable shooting, the less that you are going to be worried about the "kick" or the recoil of the gun.

Follow-Up Sequence

The follow-up sequence is a 3-step process that you should do every time you fire your weapon. We are building good muscle memory in our training. So you go to the range, pull out your handgun, fire your rounds and then go straight back to the holster. Let's say you love to train and you want to be prepared for anything so you do this thousands of times. One day you are encountered with someone who is trying to kill you. Since you have practiced your draw, carried your weapon in a position to easily access it, and you know how to shoot it, let's just say you get rounds on the bad guy and he goes down. Reverting back to your training, you quickly go back to the holster. Guess what? The bad guy is still alive and shoots you from the ground! You didn't cover your target, you didn't do your follow-up sequence. I have seen dash cam videos of Officers holstering too early after a shooting and it cost them their life.

You always revert back to your training, so every single time you shoot your weapon or do a dry fire, I want you to do this three part technique. It's called a post-engagement sequence:

1) **Follow-Through:** Follow the subject to the ground (simulate following to the ground in training).

Follow-Through

2) **Cover:** Cover your target by bringing your gun in tight (not easily taken from you), and watching your target and the area around it. You may cover for a while until law enforcement arrives on scene, or if your threat has obviously been neutralized, then we can move to step # 3. Remember that your finger needs to be off of the trigger when you are covering. You may become startled and fire a round into a non-threat and you are responsible for every round that comes out of that gun. From this position, you can still shoot the target in front of you.

Cover

Scan (360 Degrees – Eyes Only)

3) Scan: Before holstering, scan the area in front of you and behind you for additional threats with your eyes only.

Practice this technique in your training and it will become second nature during a deadly force situation.

Economy of Motion

The last piece of this fundamental puzzle is to practice these techniques enough that they become second nature. After we start to become proficient in these fundamentals, the speed will come. Just remember, accuracy is always primary and speed is secondary. I see too many people shoot faster than their skill level and the result is rounds off of target.

So what is economy of motion? It's doing all of these little things efficiently. It is getting to the desired result of rounds on target with as little motion as possible. You want to get rid of bad habits and unnecessary motion that equates to time. An example would be someone who draws and sweeps the gun towards the ground and then up before acquiring their sights. I teach to come out of the holster, to the middle of the chest, punch the gun out as you are depressing the trigger and finding the sights. The stance happens before I even touch my gun.

Another part of economy of motion is starting a drill off in the low-ready position. With the low-ready position, your gun is already out and pointed in the direction of your target. I always tell my students to point it below the hands of the target because you need to be able to see what the hands are doing. In a real-life situation, this could be the position you are at because of someone threatening your life. You may not be actively shooting at the threat, but giving them verbal directions while your gun is at this position. It should be noted that you will still need to be legally justified if you are pointing your gun at someone. From this position it takes only a split second to bring the gun up and fire rounds.

Low Ready Position

Tactical Low Ready

Drills

Here are a few drills that you can do to work on these fundamentals. I don't care how good of a shooter you are, you should practice the fundamentals every single time that you shoot.

DRILL # 1: DRY FIRE SEQUENCE

1.) Post a paper target in a safe direction

2.) Make the handgun safe and return to the holster or from wherever you normally would carry (i.e. a purse).

3.) Get into the stance (weight evenly distributed, feet shoulder width apart, knees bent, waist bent, hands above waist, head upright).

4.) Draw, find your sights, pull the trigger smoothly, and dry fire one time (simulate recoil of the gun and come back on target, finding your sights)

5.) Conduct a post-engagement sequence (follow-through, cover, scan)

6.) Reset the gun (work the slide), and return to the holster

7.) Repeat 10-20 times until comfortable

This drill works on a smooth draw as well as all of the fundamentals that we have discussed. You can conduct this drill at any distance.

DRILL # 2: DRY FIRE – COMBAT SEQUENCE

1.) Post a paper target in a safe direction

2.) Make the handgun safe and return to the holster or from wherever you normally would carry (i.e. a purse).

3.) Get into the stance (weight evenly distributed, feet shoulder width apart, knees bent, waist bent, hands above waist, head upright).

4.) Do either 10 jumping jacks, 10 push-ups, 10 squats, or 5 burpees (or a combination)

5.) Draw, do not find your sights, point weapon in the direction of the target (point shooting) with both eyes open, pull the trigger smoothly, and dry fire one time (simulate recoil of the gun and come back on target, finding your sights for a follow-up if needed)

6.) Conduct a post-engagement sequence (follow-through, cover, scan)

7.) Reset the gun (work the slide), and return to the holster (or wherever you carry)

8.) Repeat 5-10 times

This drill can be completed from the ten yard line and in. It works on a quick draw, fundamentals, and point shooting under stress.

DRILL # 3: AIM SMALL/MISS SMALL DRILLS

1.) Ensure that you have an adequate backstop and post a paper silhouette target.

2.) Using a marker draw three small circles on the target (one high, one center, and one low)

3.) Make sure you have eye and ear protection

4.) Load up several full magazines

5.) Work from the 5 yard line to start

6.) Draw and fire 2 rounds on the top small dot (take your time and find your sights)

7.) Move to the 7 yard line and repeat

8.) Move to the 10 yard line and repeat

9.) Move to the 15 yard line and repeat

10.) Move to the 25 yard line and repeat

11) Reload when needed and move back to the 5 yard line and repeat this drill until you are comfortable

12.) Make sure that after every sequence you are conducting a post-engagement sequence

The point of this drill is to aim at something smaller than the entire silhouette target, so that if you are missing the small dot, you will still be making an effective shot.

DRILL # 4: SPEED DRILLS

1.) Ensure that you have an adequate backstop and post a paper silhouette target.

2.) Make sure you have eye and ear protection

3.) Load up several full magazines

4.) From the 7 yard line:

5.) Draw, find your sights, and fire 2 rounds and then move to low-ready

6.) From the low-ready position, punch out, find your sights, and fire 2 rounds

7.) Conduct a post-engagement sequence and move back to low-ready

8.) Repeat this and every time you repeat, add some speed (push the envelope!). Work on economy of motion, eliminating unnecessary movement.

9.) Repeat until you are shooting more quickly but still accurately

10.) You can also have a partner time you on a shot timer to see your progression

I also recommend the use of "dummy rounds" to diagnose problems with anticipating the recoil of the weapon. Dummy rounds can be ordered online and are very cheap but effective. Just mix dummy rounds in your magazine with live rounds or have a partner do it for you. When you fire a dummy round during a live-fire course, the gun will just go "click". Where you learn is by noticing the barrel movement when you strike the dummy round. Did you jerk the trigger? Did you anticipate the recoil and push the gun down? These are easy fixes that will get you accurate.

Chapter 3
FIXING A
MALFUNCTION

After you have started to feel more comfortable with your handgun and you have trained the fundamentals discussed in the previous chapter, we will need to move on to malfunction drills. Knowing how to clear a malfunction is a must if you are going to carry a semi-automatic handgun. Let's first discuss the types of malfunctions that may occur and some of their causes.

Failure to Fire
(level 1 malfunction)

This is the most common malfunction and usually the easiest to fix. You point your gun downrange, pull the trigger, and it goes "click". This is sometimes referred to as a "dead man's gun" because you normally only have a split second to defend yourself against a violent attack. Some of the causes of this malfunction are:

- The operator did not charge the weapon (a bullet never made it into the chamber)
- The magazine was not seated properly into the magazine well (most common)
- Bad ammunition (misfire)

Failure to Feed
(level 1 malfunction)

This is where you charge the weapon or fire the weapon, and it does not feed a round into the chamber. There are several causes of this malfunction:

- Magazine not properly seated
- Dirty gun
- Damaged magazine
- Riding the slide: when you charged the weapon you didn't release the slide and allow it to forcefully go forward, you eased the slide forward and the weapon didn't go into battery

Failure to Extract
(level 2 malfunction)

This is where it gets a little bit trickier to fix. You fire a round and instead of kicking the spent cartridge out of the gun, it gets stuck in the chamber. Usually a double feed occurs because the gun tries to feed another round into the chamber. This can occur from:

- Limp wristing: not properly supporting the gun with your wrist locked into place
- Riding the slide
- Weak spring

Squib-Load

This type of malfunction is very uncommon but it can occur. I've only seen this occur once in my career. You fire the weapon and hear a very weak "pop" sound. The weapon fails to push the projectile out of the barrel and it gets stuck. This is usually due to a bad round. Use extreme caution if this occurs. Firing another round into the blocked barrel can cause a catastrophic malfunction resulting in serious injury. I recommend keeping the weapon pointed down range for several seconds. Take the weapon apart and inspect the barrel. You can use a rod and a hammer to tap the projectile out of the barrel. If you are brand new to handguns and this occurs, I would recommend taking the weapon to a gunsmith for inspection.

Clearing Malfunctions
LEVEL 1 MALFUNCTION

To clear a level one malfunction, do the following steps:

1) **TAP the bottom of the magazine.** This ensures that the magazine is properly seated. When I say tap, what I really mean is to slap the magazine hard enough to seat it.

Tap

2) **RACK the slide.** This will load a round into the chamber and clear the chamber if there was a misfire. When you rack the slide use the "hood" technique. Use the palm of your non-dominant hand and fingers to put a hood over the rear of the slide. Be careful not to cover the ejection port of the weapon or you may cause a malfunction.

3) **Now we are READY.** Assess the situation and determine what follow-up action is needed.

Some instructors teach to "roll" the ejection port of the gun towards the ground at the same type that you rack it which allows

Rack

Ready

gravity to assist the round to exit the port. I'm good with this technique, but I like to keep it simple with most of my students by teaching the three step process which I feel is just as effective.

So the steps to clearing a level 1 malfunction are **tap – rack - ready.** If this doesn't fix the malfunction, you will need to move on to a level 2 malfunction clearance.

Once you are comfortable with the technique, I want you to add a step to your training. If you are fixing your gun in an actual life or death situation, you do not want to be a static target. So I want you to move off line as you are fixing the gun using the big step, little step technique. You first take a big step to the left or right (a shuffle type step), and follow with the other leg with a little step

Big Step

Little Step

Clearing Malfunctions
LEVEL 2 MALFUNCTION

To clear a level 2 malfunction, take the following steps:

1) Forcibly **STRIP** the magazine from the magazine well. If you have another magazine, discard this one onto the ground. If not, stick it in a pocket. You do not want to get rid of perfectly good ammo if you can help it.

2) **WORK** the slide back and forth several times. WORK, WORK, WORK!

3) **LOAD** a new magazine or the original magazine and **TAP** the bottom to ensure that it is properly seated.

4) **RACK** the slide to load the weapon.

5) Now we are **READY**. Assess the situation and determine what follow-up action is needed.

So the steps are: **Strip – Work – Load and Tap – Rack – Ready.** Move to cover to complete this action or get off line using the big step, little step method.

Here are some drills to practice clearing level 1 and level 2 malfunctions:

DRY FIRE – LEVEL 1 MALFUNCTION DRILLS

1.) Make your handgun safe and empty and do these drills with the muzzle facing a safe direction

2.) Draw and conduct a dry fire on your target (simulates a level 1 malfunction)

3.) Big step/little step while clearing the level 1 malfunction (tap, rack, ready)

4.) Repeat until comfortable.

5.) Can also be conducted with dummy rounds

While doing these drills you should be working on all of the fundamentals that we have discussed. This is a great warm-up drill.

DRY FIRE – LEVEL 2 MALFUNCTION DRILLS

1.) Make your handgun safe and empty and do these drills with the muzzle facing a safe direction

2.) Insert an empty magazine and store one empty magazine in your magazine pouch or pocket

3.) Draw and conduct a dry fire on your target

4.) Big step/little step while clearing the level 2 malfunction (Strip – Work – Load and Tap – Rack – Ready)

5.) Repeat until comfortable.

6.) Can also be conducted with dummy rounds. It should be noted that if you do not use dummy rounds you will have to press the slide release on the weapon to make the slide go forward after reloading an empty magazine for most weapons.

LIVE FIRE – LEVEL 1 MALFUNCTION DRILLS

1.) Load your magazine with a mixture of live rounds and dummy rounds (or have a buddy load it for you)

2.) Fire at your target and clear the level 1 malfunction every time that the gun goes "click"

3.) Work this drill until it becomes second nature to tap, rack, ready when your gun goes click. This could save your life!

Chapter 4
MOVING AND SHOOTING

We have to crawl before we walk, walk before we run. So moving and shooting is somewhere in between walking and running (no pun intended). It is a skill that will not be practical if you do not practice it with hundreds of rounds.

I was teaching an ambush response class for Police Officers and we were running ambush scenarios. One of the scenarios was that the Officer was sitting in a coffee shop and a subject came inside and attempted to ambush the Officer with a handgun. In training we use simunitions, which are non-lethal rounds that hurt like hell! Ninety-Nine Percent of the Officers in the training ran backwards and took cover when the shooting started, and most of them got struck several times. But one Officer, a female Officer from a small agency in North Florida, "pressed" the threat by moving and shooting towards him. This overwhelmed our role player because of her violence of action and she easily won the fight. Does it take guts? Of course, but I promise that the bad guy isn't expecting you to move towards him. Your adversary is counting on an easy target.

Should we always press the fight to the threat? Of course not. Each deadly force situation is different. With that said, we want to practice moving every direction.

Moving Forward

If we are shooting and moving forward, we must start with that good, aggressive, isosceles stance. We bring the gun up to our eyes, lock out our arms, bend our knees, and we move forward walking heel to toe. The smoother we walk, the less muzzle movement we will get. If we do not bend our knees and walk smoothly, we will be shooting all over the place. If we do not practice this technique, we will be shooting all over the place. While practicing, focus on the front sight and eliminate as much of the movement of your gun as possible.

Another tip is to walk like you are on egg shells, as light as possible. Rolling your weight on the outsides of your feet while walking heel to toe helps. While moving and shooting it will become difficult to focus on the target, your front and rear sights, and where you are walking. Place most of your focus on that front sight. Front sight in the center mass area of the threat!

Moving Backwards

If you are moving backwards you just reverse what you did with your feet moving forward. Instead of heel to toe it is toe to heel. Make sure you have a good bend in your knees and focus on that front sight. Be careful in training that if you trip your finger is out of the trigger guard. As an instructor, I walk right behind the student to keep them from falling backwards for safety reasons.

Moving Laterally

When moving from left to right or right to left, you want to do the heel to toe method that we already discussed. Here's where it gets tricky. You want to keep your feet and lower body pointed and moving towards the location you are traveling, but rotate your upper body towards the target. I like to use the tank and the turret terminology when I am teaching this method. The tank moves and stay on the tracks while the upper part (the turret) rotates where it wants to shoot.

There is a lot of discussion on whether it is more practical to move to a location, stop, and then shoot, or to move and shoot at the same time. Here is my philosophy. Each situation dictates our tactics. There will be situations where you run to cover and then shoot, and there will be situations that may require you to move and shoot at the same time. Practice both!

Chapter 5
TARGET DISCRETION

Training the Brain to Work under Stress

Pulling your gun out and using deadly force against someone is always a last resort. You should not only always abide by state and federal laws, but also use common sense. Carry _defensively_ and not offensively. If you ever do have to defend yourself with your firearm, you are responsible for every round that comes out of that gun! You have to know how to shoot accurately under stress. If you start spraying rounds at someone, the people (possibly children) behind that person are in a lot of danger!

If you go to the range and spend a lot of time shooting and working on accuracy under no stress you will still be better off than the person who doesn't practice at all. Under stress, you will probably be average at best. If I am in a life or death situation, average is unacceptable! I've got to train my mind and my body to perform under stress. How do we do that? Simple, just get the heart rate up a little bit. Do some push-ups or jumping jacks before shooting. Maybe you run fifty yards before firing at the target. We have been training this way for a long time. What we neglect to train under stress is our brain! When stress levels go up during our fight or flight response, our cognitive thinking ability goes way down, unless we train! Here are a few ways to train your brain under stress. It should be noted that some of these drills will require a range partner or firearms instructor.

DRILL # 1

Get your heart rate up doing a set if fifteen pushups or twenty jumping jacks. Run to a table where your weapon is staged. If you feel confident enough, just keep your weapon in the holster on you during the exercises. When you get to the target area (I prefer to train 10 yards and in for a majority of my training), engage the targets that your partner has set up.

Your partner should set up at least five targets. Some are shooting targets some are non-threats. Your brain has to discern which of the targets is a threat and which ones aren't under stress. Partners can set up the targets with paper weapons taped on the hands of the silhouette targets. You can also predetermine that the targets with circles or some other shapes are threats so that you have to decide to shoot or not shoot after examining the targets. You can do the same with designated numbers or colors. I like to put these items near the hands since that is where the threat usually comes from.

After you are comfortable with this drill, run a timer and work on doing this drill faster. Adding a timer to any shooting activity always adds stress. You and your partner can also compete for the fastest time which also adds a level of stress.

DRILL # 2

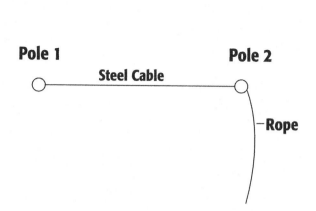

I like to run a moving target drill with my training. Most people never get a chance to use moving targets, but they add a layer of stress and cognitive thinking that most training lacks to provide. They are fairly simple to set up. Here is a diagram of a moving target system that I built in front of the berm:

All you need is a berm to shoot at. Put two polls in the ground with an eye hole on each. The polls should be at least 30 feet apart, longer is preferred. The one I built was about 50 feet in length between the polls. Run a cable tightly between the two polls. To create the moving targets all you need is another eye hole on one of your polls, some shower curtain clips to hold up your cardboard, and some thin rope to connect to the cardboard and through the eye hole. I like to make a shooting lane with barrels so that you cannot see what is coming. Your partner sets up the targets and then gets on the rope. The partner asks if you are ready and then pulls the rope, pulling the cardboard past you with the targets attached.

Here is where this can be progressive. You can speed it up. You can add more targets. You can add balloons and call out a color. You can add weapons to the hands of the silhouette targets. You can call out "two to the body and one to head of each target". The possibilities are endless. You can also induce stress before moving the targets by having the shooter do pushups or some type of exercise to get the heart rate up.

For safety, the person pulling the rope should not go in front of the firing line and should always pull from behind the shooter.

DRILL # 3: EL PRESIDENTE

This drill has been around for a while. We do this drill at most of my training. It works on teaching the shooter to engage multiple targets quickly and accurately. It teaches a fast reload and also to do all of these things under stress. Here is how it works:

The shooter faces away from the berm. There are three targets set up. I like to run this from the seven yard line. You can either set up 8 inch steel plates (I recommend using frangible ammo), or you can use paper targets. Set your targets up three yards apart. When I use the silhouette targets I make the scoring area smaller, like an 8x8 inch square on the chest. The shooter will have a holstered handgun loaded with six rounds, and an extra magazine with six rounds inside. When the timer starts the shooter will turn, then draw, and fire two rounds on each target. The shooter will complete a reload and fire two more rounds per target. Each round missed adds five seconds to the total time to emphasize accuracy over speed.

You can run this drill and compete against yourself or other people. You can run several variations of this drill: One to the body and one to the head on each target, all headshots, or even start the drill from the seated position on a chair and then stand and shoot. Either way that you run it, this drill demands speed and accuracy!

Chapter 6
HOW TO MAKE YOUR TRAINING DAY PRODUCTIVE

Quality over Quantity

How do we get the most out of practice? With training time being at a premium, how can we maximize our results? One word: Progressive! I am a firm believer in progressive training. If I had a dime for every time I was on a range with the guy who was doing rapid fire and hitting everything but the target I would be sipping Pina-coladas on an island somewhere (slightly exaggerated).

We have to crawl before we walk, walk before we run, and then, finally, we run. Even if we have done the advanced techniques dozens of times, we should always start our training with fundamentals.

I like to start each training day with a safety briefing. I read the safety rules and have them fresh in my mind. I start my day dry. Doing aim-small, miss small drills on a small dot in the middle of the paper silhouette targets until I feel like I am ready to move on. This gets me warmed up. I may do ten, I may do fifty, depends if I am having a good day or not. I do a few of these dry drills from the five yard line and move all the way back to the twenty five yard line. While I am doing these dry fires, I will work a level 1 malfunction drill in between to master that skill as well. This also sets the gun back up for the next dry fire. I do half of the dry fires from the holster and half from the tactical low-ready position.

Next, I burn through about fifty rounds. I shoot them nice and slow (no rapid fire). I work on sight alignment, trigger press, focusing on the front sight, my grip, my stance, my breathing, my trigger finger placement, and all of the fundamentals that make me a good shooter. I shoot some rounds from the five yard line and move back firing at the seven, ten, fifteen, and twenty five yard line. When a reload comes, I hit it hard! I work it like my life depends on it, because it does.

Now I have crawled, I can start walking. I load up my mags and start adding some speed to my training. Now I fire two rounds at a time (double tap) as quickly and as accurately as possible. I move from the seven to the ten yard line, then the fifteen yard line, and last the twenty five yard line. I work the reloads hard and continue to work on my fundamentals and speed. I push the envelope. I find out what works and what doesn't work. I think about economy of motion, doing as little as possible to achieve the same result. I ask questions, "how can I shorter my draw time", or "how can fire faster without jerking the trigger or throwing the second round".

I burn through those fifty rounds, I take a break, time for 50 more! This time I run a few drills. A few like el' presidente or a numbers drill will do. A numbers drill is ran with a partner. You draw numbers inside of squares on your targets and your partner calls out which numbers to shoot and in which order. These work my skills and get my brain working.

Now time to kick it up a notch, now time to run (literally). I like to get my heart rate up and then double tap from the seven yard line. I'll move and shoot, shoot from cover, reload under stress, add a timer, multiple targets, shoot and no shoot targets, and anything that makes me better under stress. This is running. I don't start this way, I end this way. And do I pick up where I left off last time? No! I return back to the fundamentals every single time to maximize my training day.

Why does this work? Because under a lot of stress, such as what you will be in during a gunfight, we will always return to what we have trained the most. Do I want to rapid fire without hitting anything? Do I want to spray and pray? No sir! I want to do the fundamental techniques that make me fast and accurate. I've trained these thousands of times and so I know what I will do when the poo hits the oscillator. I remain *fast, accurate,* and *focused* during my training and this is how I will perform when my life or someone else's life is on the line.

I hope this books adds value to you as a shooter and as an everyday carrier. I ask that you please pass this information on to those who need it as it could save their life. I cannot stress to you enough to carry defensively and not offensively. Stay up to date with your state laws that govern the use of deadly force. Don't forget to use common sense, shooting someone should not be something that any of us wants to do, it is a last resort option. Lastly, practice the fundamentals every single time you train. Stay safe out there!

For more tips and drills or to join a class,
please visit my website, www.focusedfiretraining.org.

@FOCFIRETRAINING

@ FOCUSED_FIREARMS_TRAINING

Made in the USA
Monee, IL
28 December 2020